Make a

Wind-Powered Car

by Meg Gaertner

NORWOOD HOUSE PRESS

Norwood House Press
P.O. Box 316598
Chicago, Illinois 60631

For information regarding Norwood House Press, please visit our website at:
www.norwoodhousepress.com or call 866-565-2900.

© 2019 by Norwood House Press.

LIBRARY OF CONGRESS CATALOGING-IN-PUBLICATION DATA

Names: Gaertner, Meg, author.
Title: Make a wind-powered car / by Meg Gaertner.
Other titles: Make a wind powered car
Description: Chicago, Illinois : Norwood House Press, [2018] | Series: Make your own: make it go! | Includes bibliographical
    references and index.
Identifiers: LCCN 2018005353 (print) | LCCN 2018003230 (ebook) | ISBN 9781684041947 (ebook) | ISBN 9781599539225 (hardcover
    : alk. paper)
Subjects: LCSH: Alternative fuel vehicles--Juvenile literature. | Wind power--Juvenile literature. | Handicraft--Juvenile literature.
Classification: LCC TL216.5 (print) | LCC TL216.5 .G34 2018 (ebook) | DDC 629.22/9--dc23
LC record available at https://lccn.loc.gov/2018005353

312N—072018
Manufactured in the United States of America in North Mankato, Minnesota.

Contents

Creating energy from wind is good for the environment.

CHAPTER 1

All about Wind

Since ancient times, people have used wind as a source of **energy**. It has been used to power many things, such as ships. The earliest picture of a sail appears in Egyptian art made approximately five thousand years ago. New findings say ancient humans may have been sailing for hundreds of thousands of years. Sailors today still turn the **kinetic energy** of wind into the kinetic energy of their moving ships.

Wind power can be used for more than just sailing. Long ago, people used wind to pump water or to grind grain for food. Today, people use wind **turbines** to make electricity that can power homes. Now scientists are testing to see if wind can be used to power other things, such as cars. Using common household items, you can make a wind-powered car that will help you understand how full-size wind-powered cars work.

From light breezes to tornadoes, all winds form the same way. Wind is made up of moving air **molecules**. Air molecules include water vapor and other gases. Sometimes these molecules bunch up together in one area. This creates high **air pressure**. A place where

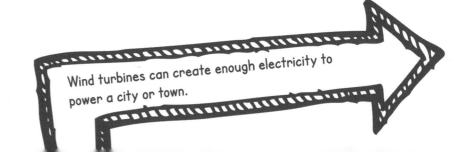

Wind turbines can create enough electricity to power a city or town.

air molecules are more spread out has lower air pressure. Air flows from places of high air pressure to places of low air pressure. This movement of air molecules is what we recognize as wind.

Wind energy is a type of **renewable energy**. This means we will never run out of it. Scientists are studying types of renewable energy to see if they can take the place of nonrenewable energy. Nonrenewable energy is energy that comes from sources Earth will run out of one day. Coal, oil, and gas are types of nonrenewable energy.

The gasoline currently used to power cars is a nonrenewable energy source. The world will run out of gasoline at some point.

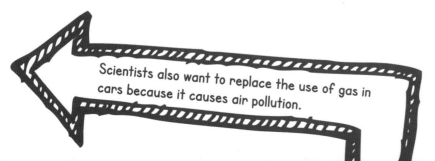
Scientists also want to replace the use of gas in cars because it causes air pollution.

But scientists are working on cars that do not run on gasoline. Today, many cars run on electricity. These cars have a **battery** that can be charged similar to how people charge their cell phones. People can plug their electric cars into charging stations.

Scientists and carmakers have already made one car model that runs completely on wind power. This car has wind turbines that collect wind and turn it into electrical energy for the car. Other **hybrid** cars combine wind turbines with batteries that use electricity. The small car that you make will run on wind power alone.

Parts of an Electric Car

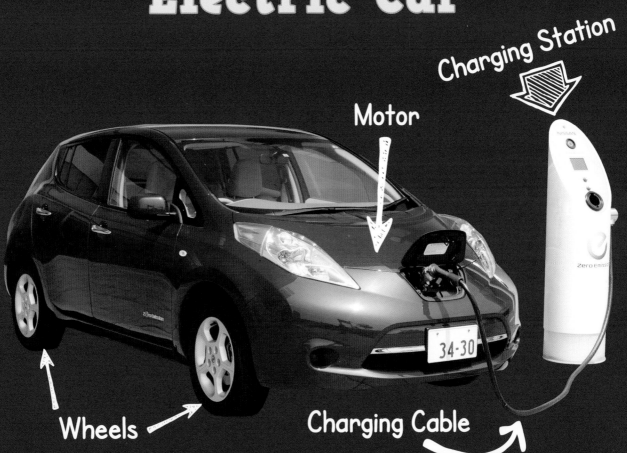

Charging Station

Motor

Wheels

Charging Cable

Real wind-powered cars don't have sails, but model wind-powered cars do.

Making a Wind-Powered Car

A model wind-powered car has sails like a boat. The frame of the car has similar features to a real car. The base of the car should be sturdy so it can hold up in the wind. It should also be lightweight. Then less wind will be needed to move it. Cardboard is an example of a material that is both sturdy and lightweight.

The base of the car will be connected to **axles**. The wheels of the car will turn around these rods. The axles need to be thin enough to fit into the center of each wheel. Drinking straws are thin and smooth. These will make good axles for your car. The wheels need to be ring-shaped. It is important that the wheels be smooth. This will reduce the effect of **friction** on the car. Friction is a force that exists any time two objects rub against each other. Friction slows moving objects down. In the case of a wind-powered car, the more friction there is, the more wind is needed to make the car move. Using smooth wheels that roll easily will help the car move faster. Round beads or ring-shaped hard candies can be used as the wheels of your car.

Without axles, the wheels of a car would not be able to move.

A model wind-powered car also needs something to catch the wind. Then it will turn the wind's energy into the car's movement. A sail connected to the car by a **mast** will catch the wind. The mast

Your wind-powered car will be fast, but not as fast as a real car.

must be strong enough to hold up the sail. It also needs to be sturdy enough to not flop over in the wind. A craft stick will work as the mast.

Like the mast, the sail should be both lightweight and sturdy. If the sail is too floppy or loose, the wind might rush right past it.

Paper might not be sturdy enough in the wind. Cardboard is sturdy, but it is also heavier and might weigh the car down too much. Thicker paper such as cardstock is both light and strong.

The shape of the sail will affect its ability to catch the wind. The angle of the sail, either toward or away from the wind, will also matter. Since ancient times, shipbuilders have experimented with different shapes and angles. Early sailors worked with square sails. Your wind-powered car will use a square sail. The flat, square shape has a large surface area that will catch a lot of wind in order to move the car.

Many ships use more than one sail. Once you build your car using a square sail, you can experiment with adding more sails.

You can also try a different sail shape to see how your car will move differently.

Finally, a wind-powered car needs wind to move. This wind could be as small as your own breath. It could be the wind outside. It could also come from a box fan inside.

To make a wind-powered car, first create the frame of the car by attaching the wheels and axles to the base. Then, attach the mast and the sail to the car. Finally, place the car in front of the source of wind. Then watch it move!

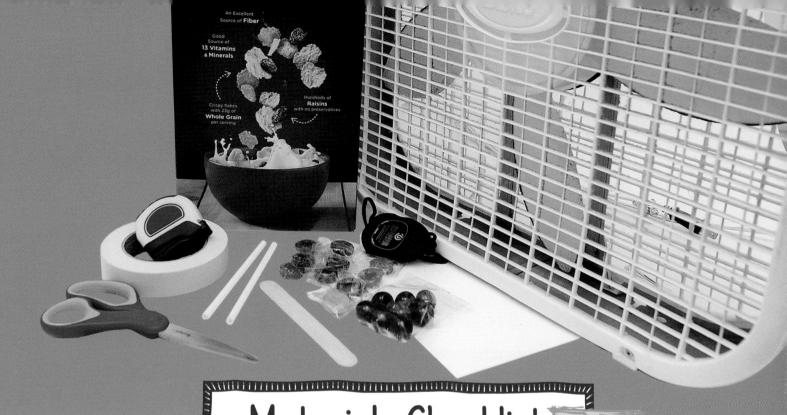

Materials Checklist

- ✓ **Empty cereal box**
- ✓ **2 straws without the bendy part**
- ✓ **1 sheet of cardstock**
- ✓ **Ring-shaped hard candies or round beads**
- ✓ **1 large craft stick**
- ✓ **Scissors**
- ✓ **Masking tape**
- ✓ **Stopwatch (optional)**
- ✓ **Measuring tape (optional)**
- ✓ **Box fan**

19

Ask an adult if you need help using scissors.

CHAPTER 3

Make It Go!

Now that you know how wind-powered cars work, let's put our knowledge to use and build one!

1. Take the cereal box and cut out a rectangle 3 inches (8 cm) wide by 4 inches (10 cm) long. The two shorter ends should be shorter than the straws.

2. Fold the rectangle in half so the two long edges are equal. Cut a small opening in the center of the folded edge. Make sure the cut is big enough to fit the craft stick.

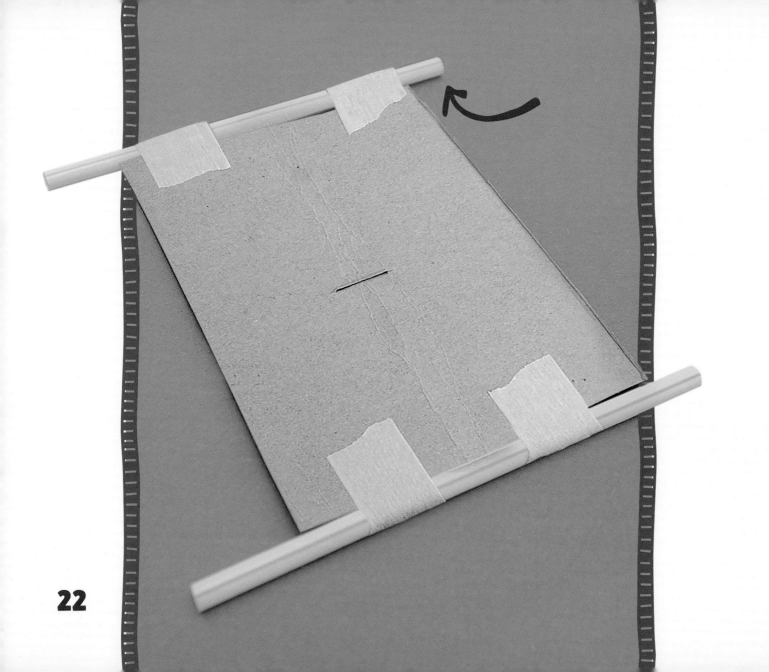

3. Unfold the rectangle. Tape a straw along each of the short edges of the rectangle. The ends of the straws should go beyond the rectangle.

4. Take four beads or candy pieces. Slide one bead or candy onto each end of the straws. Tape off each end so the beads or candies do not fall off. You have made the frame for your car.

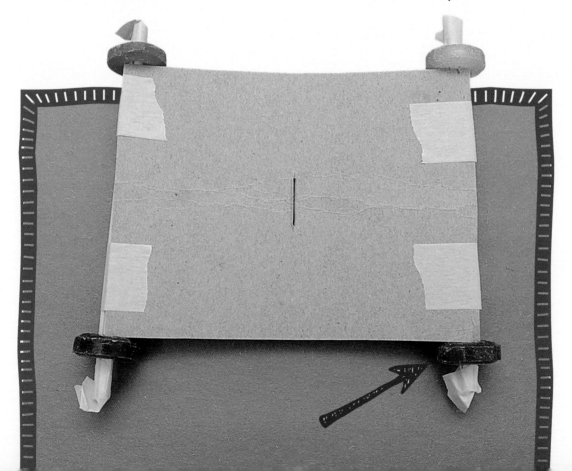

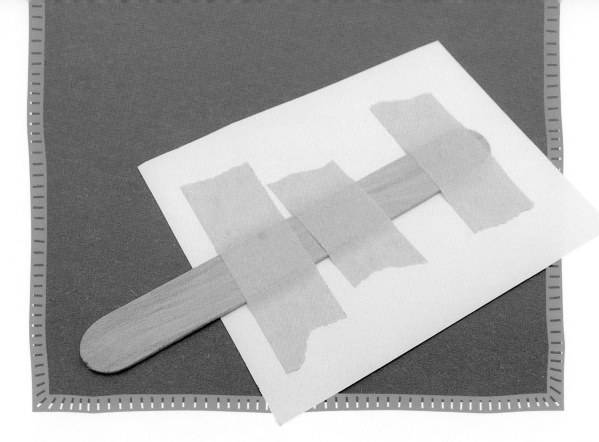

5. Create your sail. Take the sheet of cardstock and cut a rectangle, 5 inches (13 cm) tall by 3 inches (8 cm) wide. Tape one end of the craft stick to the cardstock rectangle.

6. Stick the other end of the craft stick into the opening in your frame.

Tape the craft stick in place if necessary.

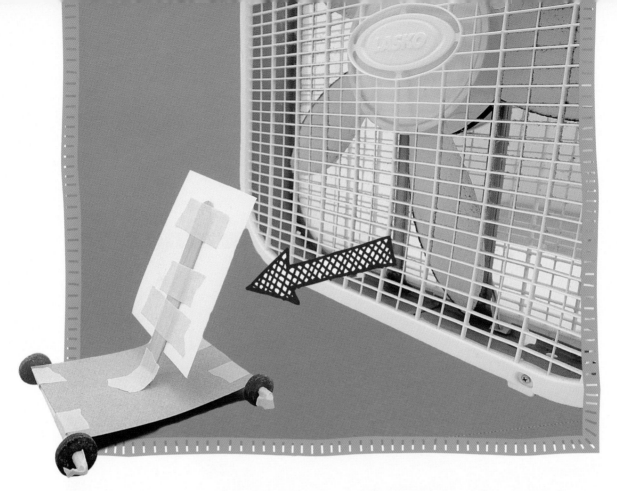

7. Put the car in front of the box fan. Turn on the fan and watch the car go!

8. Use measuring tape to see how far the car can go. Use a stopwatch to see how long it takes the car to go a certain distance.

Make It Better!

Congratulations! You built a wind-powered car. Now see if there are ways to improve it. Use any of these changes and see how they improve your wind-powered car.

- The sail in this car is a rectangle. What other shapes could you try to improve the sail? Which shape catches the wind best?

- How would changing the size of the sail change the car's movement? Does a big sail work better or worse than a small sail?

Can you think of any ways that you could improve or change your wind-powered car to work better?

Glossary

air pressure (AIR PRESH-ur): The amount of force that air molecules cause by being bunched up in a certain area.

axles (AK-suhls): Rods around which wheels turn.

battery (BAT-uh-ree): A container that stores energy by being charged with electricity.

energy (EN-ur-jee): The ability to do work.

friction (FRIK-shuhn): A force that slows down objects that rub against each other, turning the objects' kinetic energy into heat.

hybrid (HYE-brid): Combining two or more different elements.

kinetic energy (ki-NET-ik EN-ur-jee): The energy of moving objects.

mast (MAST): The pole that holds up a sail.

molecules (MOL-uh-kyools): One of the smallest pieces of matter that anything can be broken into.

renewable energy (ri-NOO-uh-buhl EN-ur-jee): Energy from sources that will never run out or be used up.

turbines (TUR-bines): Machines with blades that can be turned by wind or water passing through them.

For More Information

Books

Linda Ivancic, *What Is Wind?* New York: Cavendish Square, 2016. Students learn about the science behind wind through graphs and activities.

Michael J. Caduto, *Catch the Wind, Harness the Sun.* North Adams, MA: Storey Publishing, 2011. This book explains how renewable energy works and provides related science projects for kids to do.

Tara Haelle, *Energy Exchange.* Vero Beach, FL: Rourke, 2017. This book describes where energy comes from and how it moves from one form to another.

Websites

Kids and Energy (kids.esdb.bg/wind.html) This website explains how wind forms and how people can use wind energy to generate electricity.

National Geographic Kids: Earth Day (kids.nationalgeographic.com/explore/celebrations/earth-day/#earth-day-cleanup.jpg) This article introduces students to conservation and the different ways they can help protect nature.

PBS Kids: Blowing in the Wind (pbskids.org/video/scigirls/1434938690) In this video, students learn about renewable energy and the science of wind farms.

Index

About the Author

Meg Gaertner is a children's book author and editor who lives in Minnesota. When not writing, she enjoys dancing and spending time outdoors.